NORTH EAST SCOTLAND

Edited by Lynsey Hawkins

First published in Great Britain in 2003 by
YOUNG WRITERS
Remus House,
Coltsfoot Drive,
Peterborough, PE2 9JX
Telephone (01733) 890066

All Rights Reserved

Copyright Contributors 2003

HB ISBN 1 84460 118 8
SB ISBN 1 84460 119 6

FOREWORD

Young Writers was established in 1991 as a foundation for promoting the reading and writing of poetry amongst children and young adults. Today it continues this quest and proceeds to nurture and guide the writing talents of today's youth.

From this year's competition Young Writers is proud to present a showcase of the best poetic talent from across the UK. Each hand-picked poem has been carefully chosen from over 66,000 'Hullabaloo!' entries to be published in this, our eleventh primary school series.

This year in particular we have been wholeheartedly impressed with the quality of entries received. The thought, effort, imagination and hard work put into each poem impressed us all and once again the task of editing was a difficult but enjoyable experience.

We hope you are as pleased as we are with the final selection and that you and your family will continue to be entertained with *Hullabaloo! North East Scotland* for many years to come.

Contents

Andover School, Brechin
- Ryan Mackie — 1
- Dale McLeish — 2
- Kirstin Sherret — 3
- Glenn Jackson — 4

Borrowfield Primary School, Montrose
- Steven Keay — 5
- Rebekah Penman — 6
- Andrew Reid — 7
- Chloe McFarlane — 8
- Dean Hampton — 9
- Jack Rodger — 10
- Rebecca Mearns — 11
- Jodi Wilson — 12
- Michaela McGettigan — 13
- Kirsty Cargill — 14
- Drew Burness — 15

Carlogie Primary School, Carnoustie
- Sarah Harrison — 16
- Calum Forteath — 17
- Richard Bowman — 18
- Nathan Bowles — 19
- Stephen Quinn — 20

Colliston Primary School, Arbroath
- Ben McGinnis — 21
- Drew Gibb — 22
- Robyn McLean — 23
- John Gray — 24
- Jayde Gibson — 25
- Jo McKenzie — 26
- Alice Doyle — 27
- Colin McNaught — 28

April Shepherd	29
Fraser Gray	30
Katherine Ferrie	31
Amie Raffan	32
Craig Mitchell Ross	33
Miles Riley	34
Rebecca Corner	35
Elizabeth Webster	36

Crathes Primary School, Banchory

Katie Heath	37
Charles Booth	38

Drummoak Primary School, Banchory

Heather Robertson	39
Corrie Robertson	40
Eva Milne	41
Tom Robertson	42
Helena Fimpel	43
Liam Collie	44
Anna Hutchison	45
Grant Emslie	46
Danielle Ewing	47
Matthew Hudson	48
Elliott Warren	49
Michelle Stephen	50
Jake Malcolm	51
Paul Forbes	52
Calum Barrack	53

Fettercairn Primary School, Fettercairn

Christina Robertson	54
Michael Kelly	55
Charlotte Phipps	56
Lewis Hood	57
Cameron Shaw	58
Nicole Smith	59

Vicky Arthur	60
Samantha Farquharson	61
Rachel Donaldson	62
Rachael Farguharson	63
Lewis Wright	64
Sarah Middleton	65
Lucy Garvie	66
David Bailes	67
Vikki Reid	68
Andrew Melvin	69
Ryan Taylor	70
Kieran Glen	71
Karen Slesser	72
Zoë Kirkham-Mowbray	73
Kirsty Wright	74

Finzean Primary School, Finzean

Laura Boyle	75
Kathryn Christie	76
Katharine Pattinson	77
Rebecca Maher	78
Jack Easen	79
Bruce Jamieson	80
Calum Bell	81
Lauren Duncan	82
Rachel Lawson	83
Adèle Fraser	84
Ross Fazakerley-Guy	85
William Pattinson	86
Alistair Ross	87
Callum Christie	88
Andrew Littlejohn	89
Corrie Collander	90
Rory Farquharson	91

Hayshead Primary School, Arbroath

Alexander Park	92
Kyle Geddes	93

Jordan Donaldson	94
Daniel McArdle	95
Alan Tallis	96
Jade Williamson	97
Kerry Louise Taylor	98
Josephine Dalziel	99
Jamie Green	100
Kayleigh Ross	101
Jordan Tasker	102
Stacie Yeats	103
Caroline Watt	104
Marc Walker	105
Aimee Scott	106
Hayley Muldoon	107
Conor Alexander Warren	108
Scott Webster	109
Kara McLean	110
David Kelbie	111

Kinloch Primary School, Carnoustie

Jade Anderson Hamilton	112
Kirsty Strachan	113
Sonya Finlayson	114
Cara Steven	115

Muirfield Primary School, Arbroath

Rebecca Anne Crabb	116
Rebekah-Jo Proctor	117
Nicole-Jayne Robertson	118
Samantha McLaren	119
Darren Muldoon	120
Robbie McKenzie	121
Daniel Thomas Reid	122
Kevin Stewart	123
Charis Skea	124
Thomas Irvine	125
Steven Robert Boyd	126

Sam Ellis	127
Mitch Gillespie McDonald	128
Scott Donald	129
Jodie Lana Noble	130
Ryan Burnett	131
Bryony Joy Tait	132
Calum Robert Grant	133
Kelly-Louise Jamieson	134
Naomi Myles	135

St Ninian's Primary School, Dundee

Lloyd Ferguson	136
Jamie Bray	137
Ruth Dundas	138
Jacqueline Martinez	139
Yazmin Hodgson	140
Jemma Esposito	141
Kayesha Howett	142
Danielle Curran	143
Adam Barclay	144
Alan Muhiddin	145
Jamie Mackay	146
Lewis Toshney	147
Rebecca McDonald	148
Josh Forrester	149

Stracathro Primary School, Inchbare by Brechin

Charlotte Eggo	150
Innes Cuthill	151
Keenan Smith	152
Shaney Allan	153
John Dalgarno	154
Laura Cuthill	155
Gareth Middleton	156
Callum Leask	157
Jenny August	158
Emma Ewen	159

Alice McKenzie-Hodge	160
Linzi Box	162
Rima Puthu	163
Imogen Sherrit	164
Ruari Box	166
Eve Anderson	167

The Poems

THE SOLDIER

Marching along
Arms as straight as rulers
Legs as stiff as frosty poles
Marching along
Ears like a spy
Listening for trouble
Marching along
As tired as a sleepy baby
Feet like heavy weights
Eyes like footballs
Watching for the enemy
Marching along
Thinking of tasty food.

Ryan Mackie (8)
Andover School, Brechin

THE GLADIATOR

Standing
Waiting
For the animals to come out
Panicking
Butterflies in his tummy
Heart beating faster
Waiting
Shaking
Tummy rumbling
Just waiting
For the fight to begin.

Dale McLeish (8)
Andover School, Brechin

THE WIND

Mad
Roaring down the hill
Smashing gates
Knocking bins down
Turning umbrellas inside out
Moaning at doors
Screeching at the windows
Angry at the chimney pots
Howling at trees
Whoosh.

Kirstin Sherret (8)
Andover School, Brechin

GALE WARNING

Fences falling down
Doors slamming
Leaves whirling
TVs going fizzy
Cars tipping over
Grain blowing from the stalk
Grasses swaying
Trees crashing to the ground
Chimneys smashing
On the pavement.

Glenn Jackson (8)
Andover School, Brechin

CELEBRATE A FRIEND

My promise of friendship

I want to be friends with you
Till my bike rides itself
Till all teachers are robots
Till the sun explodes.

If we are friends
I will share my sweets with you
I will come up for you every day
I will lend you my pens.

I will give you
The first skate on my skateboard
And my last piece of birthday cake
And I will give you . . .
The first shot of my fishing rod
And the last hook.

I will like you . . .
More than a king-size Galaxy
More than the last red Smartie
And more than anything.

Steven Keay (9)
Borrowfield Primary School, Montrose

FIVE WAYS TO CELEBRATE

You can punch the air
Like a rocket taking off to space.

You can let off fireworks
Like a bird flying up to the tallest tree.

You can rent a video
Like a movie in the cinema.

You can sing like a pop star
On Top of the Pops.

You can have fun and enjoy yourself
Like a few children playing games.

Rebekah Penman (10)
Borrowfield Primary School, Montrose

CELEBRATE A FRIEND

A promise of friendship

I want to be friends with you
Till all teachers are robots
Till the sun blows up
Till we live on the moon.

If we are friends
I will come up for you every night
I will lend you my gel pens
I will let you be my partner in gym.

I will give you
The first shot of my fishing rod
And my last piece of birthday cake.

I will like you
More than a king-size Galaxy
More than a green Smartie
And more than anything.

Andrew Reid (10)
Borrowfield Primary School, Montrose

CELEBRATE A FRIEND

A Promise of friendship

I want to be friends with you
Till blackcurrant juice turns green.
Till the moon turns red
Till the world turns small.

If we are friends
I will let you ride my bike
I will let you have my chocolate.

I will give you my first sticker
I will give you my book to read
And my last Rolo.

I will like you
More than chocolate biscuits
More than comics
And more than my pogo stick.

Chloe McFarlane (10)
Borrowfield Primary School, Montrose

SILVER

S ilver hair gel sparkling in the sun
I see the silver moon at night like diamonds
L ike shiny beetles scuttling along the ground
V ases of flowers silver in the moonlight
E lectric eels like lightning forks
R obots' silver metal like frosted trees.

Dean Hampton (9)
Borrowfield Primary School, Montrose

SILVER

Big, strong, metal robot
Shining in the sun.

Silver paint glittering
In the moonlight.

Gleaming hard tin foil
Like metal's bent.

Cold and sparkling metal
Like a mirror shining on the sun.

Big silver buttons
Like an army of silver men.

Small silver gel pens
Like silver fillings in your mouth.

Jack Rodger (9)
Borrowfield Primary School, Montrose

SILVER

Silver is like a tiara,
Small but shiny,
Like a star-sparkling sky.

Silver is like water,
Glistening,
Like the sun's bright light.

Silver is like stars,
Glittering in the moonlight,
Like never before.

Silver is like paint,
Shining in the sun,
Like a splat of real silver.

Rebecca Mearns (10)
Borrowfield Primary School, Montrose

SILVER

Silver is like metal
That's bright and shiny,
Like the silver moon
Gleaming in the sky.

Silver is like a bunch of stars
Grouped together at night,
Like a family of
Little bunnies.

Silver is like a glittery robot
Reflecting on the cold dew,
Like a sunbeam
Reaching from the sky.

Silver is like a sparkling necklace
Newly-bought from a shop,
Like a trophy just been polished.

Jodi Wilson (9)
Borrowfield Primary School, Montrose

CELEBRATE A FRIEND

A Promise Of Friendship

I want to be friends with you
Till my bottle explodes everywhere.

If we are friends
I will give you some of my sweets
I will give you some cola at my home.

I will give you
First shot on my scooter
And my last bite of cake.

I will like you more than my sister
I will like you more than my chocolate sundae
I will like you more than the world.

Michaela McGettigan (9)
Borrowfield Primary School, Montrose

CELEBRATE

I celebrate
The sight of children playing
Happily together in the park,
Like a flock of birds looking for food.

I celebrate
The sound of birds chirping
In the trees,
Like a squeaky door.

I celebrate
The feel of a foam bath,
Like a snow bath.

I celebrate
The taste of strawberries and cream
In a bowl,
Like red and white scribbles.

I celebrate
The memory of when I first met Chloe
Because she is a friend indeed!

Kirsty Cargill (10)
Borrowfield Primary School, Montrose

CELEBRATE A FRIEND

A Promise of friendship

I want to be friends with you
Till I hit a golf ball around the world
Till the world ends
Till I get £100,000.

If we are friends
I will come up for you every day
I will give you my CDs
I will give you my PC if I die
And my last Linkin Park CD.

I will like you
More than my mum
More than my PS2
More than Scary Movie 2.

Drew Burness (10)
Borrowfield Primary School, Montrose

WHAT IS AMETHYST?

Amethyst is velvet, royal and rich,
Magical powers, crystal and glass,
Snoozy, gentle and calm,
Sparkles and glistens, reflecting the sea.
Amethyst is beautiful, graceful and gleams.
Amethyst sparkles like the sun, moon and stars.
It's a millennium colour.
Lovely and shiny, giving lots of joy.

Sarah Harrison (11)
Carlogie Primary School, Carnoustie

WHAT IS AMETHYST?

Amethyst is a royal mineral, small and cold,
Amethyst is a sparkly mineral, jagged, sleepy and unwoken,
Amethyst is calm, rich and mysterious,
Amethyst is a crystal which is shiny in the starlight,
Amethyst is like lavender, but is not smooth-like,
Amethyst is the most beautiful crystal the Earth will ever see.

Calum Forteath (11)
Carlogie Primary School, Carnoustie

WHAT IS AMETHYST?

Amethyst is shiny, like glistening water from a mountain stream
It is as colourful as country heather
It can be as jagged as a knife and as smooth as a grape
Amethyst is as royal as the Queen in its own right
The sleeping stone will never wake for it is always well hidden.

Richard Bowman (11)
Carlogie Primary School, Carnoustie

WHAT IS AMETHYST?

Amethyst is beautiful,
Amethyst is calm,
Amethyst is a sleepy colour,
Amethyst is the jewel on the Queen's crown,
Amethyst sparkles like the moon,
Amethyst is a crystal, so shiny and bright,
Amethyst is such a magical sight.

Nathan Bowles (11)
Carlogie Primary School, Carnoustie

WHAT IS AMETHYST?

Amethyst is sleepy
Amethyst is royal
Amethyst is magnificent
Amethyst is loyal
With layers of history
What holds beneath?
The magic of amethyst
Like a purple chief
A millennium colour
That glistens with light
The goddess of darkness
So brilliantly bright.

Stephen Quinn (11)
Carlogie Primary School, Carnoustie

FUTURE

Into the future I see
My crystal ball is only wee
I see you and a lady having tea
On a moonlit balcony.

She's got brown hair
She's single - that's rare
Love and war, it's not fair
Oh no you fall over
That looked sore
Have a nice time, do a dare.

Into the future I see
My crystal ball is only wee
We don't need it anymore
Now we've got . . .

Technology!

Ben McGinnis (11)
Colliston Primary School, Arbroath

ANIMALS

Animals come in different shapes and different sizes,
Like a puppy, soft and cuddly.
Some animals aren't like that.
Some are fierce and ugly.
Some can't come out of water,
Like a fish or a dolphin.
Some can go out and in water,
Like a crocodile.
Some come out only at night,
Like an owl
But I only have one favourite animal
And that's a dog.

Drew Gibb (9)
Colliston Primary School, Arbroath

CATS

Cats are cute and cuddly things
Some will scratch and some will bite
Some are spotted black and white
If you go too close to some
They will give you a bleeding thumb
Some like some people and some like you
Some drink milk and some drink out of the loo
They eat whatever you give them
Some like me but I like all of them.

Robyn McLean (10)
Colliston Primary School, Arbroath

I'M A MOUSE

Creep, creep, creep under the floorboards I go
I'm only a wee mouse not an inch from the floor
I'm going on a dander all on my own
Where am I going?
Across the living room plains
Och I'll take a wander o'er kitchen moors
And into cheese cupboard county
Stilton, mozzerella, cheddar!
Which one will I choose?
Cheddar!

John Gray (11)
Colliston Primary School, Arbroath

THE BUTTERFLIES

I have a butterfly collection
They stand and stare at me
I keep them in a box all day
Then take them out for tea.

I take them to McDonald's
I take them to KFC
I take them to the seaside
To see what we can see.

I can see whales swimming
I can see dolphins diving
But most of what I can see
Are the waves arriving.

But now's the time to let them go
To let them fly away
Oh no here comes a crash landing
My butterflies die today.

Jayde Gibson (11)
Colliston Primary School, Arbroath

SNOW

Snow, snow, snow
Falling from the sky
It looks amazing
It looks wonderful.

When you look around the playground
You find snow galore
The snow is like tiny white fairies
Flying from the sky
Everybody loves the snow
Especially if it becomes heavy
Then we get a day off school!

Jo McKenzie (11)
Colliston Primary School, Arbroath

SEATS

I sit in my chair at school
I see the rooks sitting on a tree.
Sometimes I see grey clouds standing there
And the sky as blue as can be.

I sit at my desk at home,
I can see the wall
And the computer
Plus the door to the hall.

But the best seat of them all
Is the sofa in front of the TV!

Alice Doyle (10)
Colliston Primary School, Arbroath

POP STARS

Pop stars are famous
They get a lot of cash
And without a trace
They make a quick dash.

Driving in a fancy sports car
Just out for a spin
Off to the Brit Awards
I really hope to win.

They call my name
I've beaten the best
And all the rest,
You will see the best of me.

Colin McNaught (11)
Colliston Primary School, Arbroath

MY HAMSTER

Some people think my hamster is a pest
But I think my hamster is the best
Her name is Anastasia
I think it's a bit posh for a hamster
She sometimes bites a little
But I don't think she means to be brutal
She's a sort of creamy colour
With little, black, beady eyes
Sometimes she shudders
If she's frightened or sad
She gets out in her ball
But I don't ever put her on the table
Just in case she falls!
I think my hamster's the best.

April Shepherd (8)
Colliston Primary School, Arbroath

MY PET CAT

My cat's fur's like silk
She drinks a lot of milk,
She doesn't like noise
But she does play with toys,
She'll get chased by dogs
And she doesn't eat frogs.
She isn't very fat
But she plays with the other cat.
She's always wanting food
If she doesn't get it she'll go in a mood.
When she has a sore head
She sleeps on my bed.

Fraser Gray (9)
Colliston Primary School, Arbroath

I Want To Be A Cheerleader

I want to be a cheerleader
And jump up high,
I want to be a cheerleader
And touch the sky.
Do flips so people can catch me
Invite cool girls round for tea.
Dance around and shout with glee,
'Hey everybody! Look at me!'
I want to wear a mini skirt
And a cute wee top,
I know where you can find them -
In the cheerleading shop.
Maybe a blue outfit, or maybe green
I guarantee you,
It'll be the best you've ever seen.

Katherine Ferrie (11)
Colliston Primary School, Arbroath

A Day In The Life Of Me

I wake up in the morning
When the sun is shining bright
I get up and get dressed
I look down from my bed
And it is a mess
I get down from my bed
I put on my red tie.
I say to myself
I hear blackbirds singing
I go through for my breakfast
But I don't have enough time.
It is quarter to nine.
I hop in the car
Go down to school
We get out at quarter-past three
I go home and get my tea,
Then I feel very tired
I go to bed and rest my head.

Amie Raffan (11)
Colliston Primary School, Arbroath

HUNT

When hunting in the forest deep
I saw a bear in its sleep.
Although armed with a spear
Yet still a bear I did fear.
So I searched for something smaller
I would get the bear if I were taller.
I moved elsewhere
To find a hare
Or something that size,
A bear would be a fine prize.
I saw the tracks of wild boar
All over the forest floor
I followed them to a tree
But then the tracks I couldn't see,
They just seemed to disappear.
A new sound I could hear
A fox I saw so I gave chase
And then a bush I seemed to face,
The sly fox had gotten away
And I decided to stay
In the forest overnight
With a big lack of light
Now I will be restful
For the hunt wasn't successful.

Craig Mitchell Ross (10)
Colliston Primary School, Arbroath

Football

We start from the middle
And then I pass it back.
The ball gets driven down the wing
And now we are on an attack.

My friend takes it to the corner
And gives it a good old kick.
It is now my time to stand up tall
And score a goal for Wick.

Miles Riley (11)
Colliston Primary School, Arbroath

MY PET KITTEN

My kitten is silky, soft and black
She catches mice and sometimes a rat,
She chases the ducks and makes them quack
She's quite a naughty pussy cat.

She sleeps with me at the top of my bed,
Plays with my hair and gives me cuddles,
She wraps herself around my head
That is why I called her Snuggles.

In the morning she wakes me up
To tell me she wants to be fed,
She tries to lick stuff from my cup
But gets her cat food instead.

She sits at the window when I go for the bus
To spend the day at school,
When I get home she makes a fuss
And runs around with her ball of wool.

She sits and watches us having dinner
Hoping to get a bite,
But she doesn't get any thinner
And I can still lift her because she's light.

Rebecca Corner (10)
Colliston Primary School, Arbroath

HOLIDAY TIME

Holidays come, where shall we go?
The Big Apple - lots of shops.
Hawaii - lots of dancing girls,
Oh where shall we go?
What about France? Bonjour.
Maybe Canada with lots of bears.
Oh where shall we go?
I want to go to Egypt
But Mum fancies Italy.
Oh where shall we go?
And Dad wants to go to the desert.
My little brother wants to go to space.
Oh where shall we go?
But we all want to go to Australia
So off we go in the plane with a pain.
Now we're here let's have some fun.
Time to go home until the next holiday,
Oh where shall we go?

Elizabeth Webster (9)
Colliston Primary School, Arbroath

SNOW IN WINTER

A great glistening white sheet,
Far as the eye can see.
Up to the horizon,
Over the mountains,
Stretching down to the sea.
Snowmen glinting,
With eyes made of coal.
Pebble buttons
And a carrot nose.
Then all of this melts,
To be replaced by green.
Green grass, green bushes,
Green moss, green trees.
All of this stays,
As long as it can.
Until autumn comes.
Staining the leaves, red and gold.
Then, they gently tumble from the trees,
To be hidden by snow,
By ice and by sleet.
Back comes the ice,
That glistening white sheet.
The snowmen, the snowballs,
The sledges and skis
Oh can't winter stay?
Oh can't the leaves go?
All of the ice and the snow, snow, snow.

Katie Heath (9)
Crathes Primary School, Banchory

SUNSET

Running down the alley
Not sure what to do
The rats scatter
A window shatters
They're not through with you
He'd have liked to be friends
But this is where it all ends
He tripped, he stumbled
It was enough
There was a crack
The world went black
He hit the floor
He had no strength at all
He wanted to struggle
Chains embrace him.
There was a flash
And he felt nothing at all.

Charles Booth (11)
Crathes Primary School, Banchory

SLEDGING

Trudging on through wind and cold,
Bent and puffed, not straight and bold,
Striding on through endless snow,
Onward, upward, off I go.
Blizzards, cold and cloudy vision,
Could this be a mad decision
But there is no one out here, so
Who is going to stop me go?
Downpour, gale and drizzly sleet
With my frozen fingers meet
Helping to obstruct my way,
Maybe this is not my day.
At the top and it's all worth it,
Turn around and slide a bit,
One big push and off I go,
Then I shout and cheer and bellow
And in the midst of my excited scream
I think it's like a marvellous dream.
After that long, weary mile
Now I yell and kick the smile,
Whizzing past the great, huge trees,
Branches inches from my knees.
Who needs parks and pools and sun
To have an amazing load of fun?
People stop and turn and stare
But I'm just a hazy glare.
Round I turn and off I fall
Right beside a tree so tall.
Although I know it sounds insane,
I'll go back up and try again.

Heather Robertson (10)
Drumoak Primary School, Banchory

HENRY'S WIVES

Three Catherines, two Annes and a Jane
Were married in King Henry's reign
When he married the sixth one
He said, 'This is no fun,
I'll never get married again!'

Corrie Robertson (10)
Drumoak Primary School, Banchory

THE TROUT

A darting creature glided along the bright, shimmering water
Creating, in the miserable weather, the most wonderful reflection.
Heavy rain bounced off the river,
Hit the dirty mounds of leaves on the frozen banks.
The trout's eyes were river stones,
His flickering tail the swaying grass.
He moved slowly like a soldier coming back from war,
And peeked from the water at the shadows of bushy trees.
There was a splash far away, a diving, struggling sound.
The forest was asleep.
A creature walked with a threaded device,
Strong footsteps crashed on the sprouting grass.
A sharp hook dived like a sparkling sword.
It grabbed the poor, unhappy-looking fish,
Brought him above the water to the cold rain,
Into a small, brown basket.
He thought of good times and bad.
The trout shut his eyes and dreamt.

Eva Milne (10)
Drumoak Primary School, Banchory

THE TUDORS

Henry had a need for power
But he couldn't get on with Richard's glower,
So they went to battle on Bosworth Field
To try to make each other yield.
Henry won and became number seven
While Richard took a ride to Heaven.

Henry VIII became round and unfit,
To make him slim he'd have to lose a bit.
To wife number one he couldn't stick
And number five he gave a good, hard kick,
But number six held on longer than him
So her life at court was not nearly so grim.

Edward VI was a sickly boy,
A normal life he couldn't enjoy.
When he reached the throne
Ed was skin and bone,
Was never keen,
Died at only sixteen.

Mary I was a mean old crow
But just how mean we can never know.
She enjoyed some killing,
Victims never willing.
When she suddenly died
No one cried inside.

Elizabeth I had many strong seamen
Who sailed the seas again and again.
She loved to play a leading role
Her smile showing teeth as black as coal.
She didn't look like *our* Queen Lizzie,
Her hair was red and really frizzy.

Tom Robertson (10)
Drumoak Primary School, Banchory

WITCH

I see a dark shadow
With a stuck up chin.
I hear a cackly voice
And I say, 'What can it be?'
It's an old wrinkly witch
And she's in my house
With her black, hollow cauldron.
Out come the bloodworms
And then some slime.
She opens a spell book . . .
And I shout for Mum.

Helena Fimpel (10)
Drumoak Primary School, Banchory

THE CLOUD TRAIN

I see white clouds,
I see grey clouds
And a beautiful, crispy, crunchy one.
Suddenly a cloud bursts
Into two and more pieces.
One's black and angry,
One's huge and bumpy,
Some are tiny and round.

What's that?
Up there.
A strange-looking shape,
I think it's a train.

It's a huge stream engine
With mini puffs of smoke
Pulling five fluffy carriages
Across the sky.

Liam Collie (10)
Drumoak Primary School, Banchory

MONDAY AGAIN

My sister's complaining, something's lost,
Mum's still deciding what to wear,
Dad makes a racket in the kitchen
And it really isn't fair.

It's eight fifteen already
And I haven't even brushed my hair.
The fish food's fallen on the floor
But, really, I don't care.

My breakfast's on my clean, new skirt,
I haven't got two matching socks on,
My lace is undone, I trip and fall,
It's past the time I should have gone.

I've already fed my hungry guinea pig
And I'm just about to step out the door.
My pile of homework is under my arm
When greedy guinea squeals for more.

This is a typical Monday morning,
Not very calm as you can see.
I think it's the worst day of the week
And that is how it's meant to be.

Anna Hutchison (10)
Drumoak Primary School, Banchory

JET

I have a young dog called Jet
With a face I could never forget.
Her coat is black with a shine,
I'm amazed that something so good is mine,
She is an unbeatable pet.

She likes to play with a ball,
She comes to me when I call,
She loves to have her belly rubbed
But she's not so keen on being scrubbed,
She's the best dog of them all.

When you hear the doorbell ring
You'll hear her bark, not sing,
With a white mark on her chest
I know she's simply the best,
She should be treated like a king.

I like to take her for walks,
We play hide-and-seek on the rocks.
She's a brilliant friend,
On her I depend
And sometimes she almost talks.

I seldom see her sleep,
Never dreamless and deep.
She's always ready for tea,
The best thing that's happened to me,
I'm glad she's mine to keep.

Grant Emslie (10)
Drumoak Primary School, Banchory

DOLPHIN

See little dolphin
Leaping and jumping,
Blue as the sea
Her name is Shree.
Come little dolphin
Leaping and jumping,
Come little Shree,
Come to me.
Cute little dolphin
Leaping and jumping,
Let me stroke you,
Sparkling and blue.

You dive away,
Can't you stay?
I guess not,
I guess not.
Leaping and jumping,
Leaping and jumping.

Danielle Ewing (11)
Drumoak Primary School, Banchory

CLOUDS

I was lying in the sun,
Watching the clouds go by,
With cirrus and stratus
And cumulus too,
They are amazing shapes to see.
Wait - I see an armchair,
It's white
And fluffy
And very, very big.

Matthew Hudson (10)
Drumoak Primary School, Banchory

CLOUDS

Some are lumpy,
Some are wispy,
Some are spongy,
Some are creamy.
In the air
There are weird shapes.
One's a dog,
One's a fish.
Playing games with clouds
Is fun.

Elliott Warren (10)
Drumoak Primary School, Banchory

CLOUDS

Clouds are fluffy and soft,
Like cuddly teddy bears.
But sometimes they're hard
With sharp-looking edges.
They climb up,
Clouds upon white clouds.
Wispy and wavy,
Sometimes grey and fierce,
Then fast and clear on lovely days.

Michelle Stephen (10)
Drumoak Primary School, Banchory

CLOUDS

Big, lumpy clouds,
Wispy, bushy clouds,
Chunky, dark clouds,
Bumpy, flossy clouds,
Soft, curving clouds,
Whippy, springy clouds,
Spongy, fierce clouds,
Bright, kind clouds,
Bad, slanted clouds,
Bloated, long clouds,
Short, puffy clouds,
Fluffy, downy clouds,
Velvet, silky clouds,
Smooth, hovering clouds
Floating up above.

Jake Malcolm (10)
Drumoak Primary School, Banchory

CLOUDS

Big, bushy clouds,
Small, whippy clouds,
Long, fluffy clouds,
Dark, fierce clouds,
Hard, bumpy clouds
And light, bright clouds,
Which will I see today?

Paul Forbes (10)
Drumoak Primary School, Banchory

ICE CREAM

Ice cream, yummy
In my tummy
Little lips
Make lots of drips.
Cones and cups and crispy wafers
Fill them with my favourite flavours.
Crunch on the cone
Then munch the sprinkles,
Lick and lick
Make myself sick.
Ice cream, ice cream
I'm in a dream.

Calum Barrack (11)
Drumoak Primary School, Banchory

SCOOBIE DOOBIE DOO MY DOG

I miss Scoobie jumping up
I miss Scoobie licking me
I miss Scoobie barking all night
I miss Scoobie growling loudly
I miss Scoobie's kiss on the cheek
I miss Scoobie lots and lots
I love Scoobie Doobie Doo.

Christina Robertson (9)
Fettercairn Primary School, Fettercairn

T REX

  T yrannosaurus rex
  R uns fast
  E xtinct long ago
eX tremely dangerous.

Michael Kelly (9)
Fettercairn Primary School, Fettercairn

PONIES

Professionals galloping away
On top of hills and mountains
Neighing in time with the wind.
Your pony would be so cute,
Safe and steady.

Charlotte Phipps (9)
Fettercairn Primary School, Fettercairn

DAVID BECKHAM

David Beckham
Is a good goal scorer
Intelligent at football
Brilliant at his crosses
Excellent bender
Hammers it into the back of the net
His kicks are amazing.

Lewis Hood (9)
Fettercairn Primary School, Fettercairn

FRIENDS

F riends are helpful, friends are kind
R eally, really nice and generous
I f you don't have friends make one and don't be sad
E very time they play with you
N eed a friend, be a friend
D on't hurt people who want to be friends
S o don't be bad to people - be good.

Cameron Shaw (8)
Fettercairn Primary School, Fettercairn

FROST

Feathery and twinkling
Nippy and sharp
Like glitter
Sprinkling the garden.

Nicole Smith (9)
Fettercairn Primary School, Fettercairn

FISH

F   ins wiggle
I   see big fish and small
S   ea lions chase them
H   ope the little fishes get away.

Vicky Arthur (9)
Fettercairn Primary School, Fettercairn

THE LOST BARN OWL

The rusty, old, mouldy barn house
Is cold and wet
The windows are all smashed
The door's gone
And there are owls living there.
One is missing
It is getting dark
There he is
Asleep in the rotten hay.

Samantha Farquharson (9)
Fettercairn Primary School, Fettercairn

HARP SEALS

H iding in the cold, wet snow
A lways lying, sleeping
R ocking from side to side when it's playing
P addling in the cold water.

S nuggling into his mother's fur
E verybody likes harp seals
A lways eating their favourite food
L ovely and sweet
S mells danger if near.

Rachel Donaldson (10)
Fettercairn Primary School, Fettercairn

THE BARN OWL

In the rusty old barn
In the stack of hay
There was a little barn owl asleep
And tucked away
He didn't want to be disturbed
In his dark, dark sleep.

Rachael Farquharson (9)
Fettercairn Primary School, Fettercairn

MUM THE GREAT COOK

M y mum
U ltra skilled
M akes

T remendous things to eat
H ot porridge on cold days
E njoying everything edible.

G obbling it all up
R eads and remembers recipes
E xciting meals
A nd
T asty

C ookies are a challenge
O r amazing cakes
O ozing icing, she is the
K ing of the kitchen.

Lewis Wright (9)
Fettercairn Primary School, Fettercairn

ICE

Like stained glass
It's hard, it's hard,
Like shiny crystals
In the end it melts.

Sarah Middleton (9)
Fettercairn Primary School, Fettercairn

THE LOST CAT

The lost cat
goes out at night,
looking for its family.
It goes all over the town,
looking for its family
but never finds them.

Lucy Garvie (9)
Fettercairn Primary School, Fettercairn

IN A PERFECT WORLD

In my perfect world
there would be loads of tractors,
quads and trailers with turbo engines
that you would not have to buy.
There would be no school,
you would just know the work when you were born
and everything would be made out of chocolate.
There would be no girls or nasty dolls
but we could go up to space.
We would get a motorbike for free.
No one would have to pay for anything
not even at Christmas.
We could get food for free
and not pay at any fairs
and get free rides and free meals.
We would get fizzy pop for free, even in our taps.

David Bailes (8)
Fettercairn Primary School, Fettercairn

Autumn

Autumn is the best season of the year,
the hedgehog is eating lots and lots of food,
the leaves are the best colour of the year
as the leaves drift down to the ground.
I watch the leaves fall down to the ground
I watch the birds go to the south for the winter.

Vikki Reid (8)
Fettercairn Primary School, Fettercairn

THE FLOOD

Water gushing to the bridge
Sandbags getting put down
People rushing to the shops
The water fast flowing
Water everywhere
On the road, in the garden
Causing chaos in the streets
People panic in their houses.

Andrew Melvin (8)
Fettercairn Primary School, Fettercairn

AUTUMN

Farmers harvesting
Birds flying
Chicks learning to fly
Leaves turning gold, yellow and red
Leaves falling
Lambs running around the field
Hedgehogs curling up for the winter
Leaves blowing about
Bonfires on the hill
Birds flying in a v-shape
Birds flying south
Smelly air
Fieldmice nibbling berries
Squirrels building cashes
Squirrels getting ready for winter
Pea-viners cutting peas.

Ryan Taylor
Fettercairn Primary School, Fettercairn

AUTUMN

Leaves falling
Harvesting time
Fieldmice sleeping
Rabbits digging burrows
Hedgerows planted
And a beautiful sunset
Children playing in the leaves
Wrapped up warm
Golden corn and wheat
Geese flying south
Flowers dying
Mice eating berries
Farmers working hard
Colours everywhere
Squirrels scampering up and down
Pea-cutters, cutting peas.

Kieran Glen (8)
Fettercairn Primary School, Fettercairn

Autumn

Leaves falling all around us
Children playing
Having fun
Autumn days
Spiderwebs on trees
Children playing on the hillsides
Playing in leaves
Squirrels collecting nuts
Hedgehogs hibernating
Birds flying to hotter places
Dew on the grass
Colder days
Adults getting peace
Birds flying south in a v-shape
Dormice hibernating
Farmers harvesting.

Karen Slesser (9)
Fettercairn Primary School, Fettercairn

AUTUMN

Time to harvest all the crops
And pick all the apples
Squirrels burying food
To last all through the winter
Crunchy fallen leaves
Are all over the ground
Time for lots of conker fights
With conkers from the ground
Birds flying south
In a funny v-shape
Hedgehogs finding food
So they are fat for the winter
Autumn makes me feel good.

Zoë Kirkham-Mowbray (8)
Fettercairn Primary School, Fettercairn

Summer

Summer sun
Having fun

Deckchairs
Paddling pools

Sheep getting shaved
Out of their winter coats

Bees making honey from nectar
Butterflies buzzing

Nights getting shorter
Days getting longer.

Kirsty Wright (7)
Fettercairn Primary School, Fettercairn

THE HIGHEST HEAVEN

Dear my papa, the kindest person I've ever known,
A heart of gold and soul of peace
If I could change the past I would,
Change a lot of things but I'd change your death to life
Because I miss you like the sun misses the flower.
Like the evening misses the stars
And let me be a light to you during bad times.
You don't have the faintest clue
How many running tears there have been.
I just want you to know that I miss you and I love you!

Laura Boyle (9)
Finzean Primary School, Finzean

PLAYFUL PANDAS

Pandas, pandas they want to come and play
Their soft, long fur flowing in the air every day.
They won't stop and play,
They're as tall as a person on top of a tree.
Pandas, pandas, they're as cute as you can think.
Pandas, pandas, they'll chase you
So give them some food.
They watch out for poachers, but they have got too many tricks,
They show off their teeth.
They chew as fast as an elephant falling down a tree.
They splash in the water and get all wet
And shake you and you'll get all wet
They'll run back home and they'll snuggle up in bed.

Kathryn Christie (8)
Finzean Primary School, Finzean

My Puppy

I found him on the beach one day
All cold and wet.
He followed me home through the door
I have a brand new pet.

He let me stroke him, more and more
Till Mum came home from work.
He got my gran's balls of wool
And fell into a dark, dark cupboard.

He ran away.
He didn't come back
Then I was very upset.

When I find him, if he's sick
I'll take him to the vet.

Katharine Pattinson (9)
Finzean Primary School, Finzean

MUSTANGS NEVER WANT TO STOP

Mustangs galloping across a field of gold
They never want to stop
Here and there and everywhere
They never want to stop.

As wild as an eagle
This herd of free spirits
But still they never want to stop
Just gallop over the hills and far away.

Alas it's time to go down to the waterhole
To have a drink
And splash and splash all about
They never want to stop.

Now the rest of the day
They spend grazing away
Even though they are exhausted
They never want to stop.

Munching and crunching
With those great big jaws
But now they want to stop
To go to bed and lay down their heads.

Rebecca Maher (9)
Finzean Primary School, Finzean

MY CAT

My cat's name is Bob
He is as cuddly as a kitten
He's playful, he scratches
And is a fast runner
But a big, big fat cat
With a long, long tail
And a big furry coat and nice paws
It balances like a tree trunk.
They are loving things
To have as pets.

Jack Easen (10)
Finzean Primary School, Finzean

MY ROOM

My room is messy and hard work to clean up
It's nice and warm and very dusty
But my room is very small
With boxes under my bed
And a storage of sweets in a secret room
But no one knows where this secret place is.

My door squeaks like a little mouse in the corner
Squeak, squeak, squeak goes the door
Every morning and night
I don't know what I'm going to do with that door.

My bed is messy
I've got to tidy it up
My covers are off because I rolled around in the night
But my dad said, 'Tidy that bed up now!'
So I tidied and tidied
But still it's a mess
But at last it's done
So my dad's as happy as ever.

Bruce Jamieson (10)
Finzean Primary School, Finzean

THE MOUSE'S SUNDAY

The mouse I am talking about sleeps all night
When he gets up he gets dressed.
And because it's Sunday he wears his best.
Up the stairs he scuttles, stops and starts.
His objective is the treacle tarts.
Every hair and paw is tense, hence the leering traps.
Soon he is there, he sniffs, sniffs, sniffs the air.
There are humans around, he sniffs again and feels the ground!

The danger passed, he zips through a door, fast.
But his long tail hits a pail and makes a clang.
He rolls out of sight, oh what a fright!

Next is the kitchen.
He doesn't know which end to visit first.
He is in Heaven, there're chunks of cheese and snippets of fish
And old soggy cornflakes laid out in a dish.

Calum Bell (10)
Finzean Primary School, Finzean

SCHOOL

People talking, cheering, learning all day long
Others scared like little ants in case they get it wrong
But the others are sharpening their pencils by the end of the day
Because they are as smart as the teacher on their desk all day.

In and out school we go playing in the mud
Going *splash, splash, splash*
But some of the children watch the road
With the cars going *zoom, zoom, zoom*
And the drums are going *boom, boom, boom.*

Did you know the pencils dance when they need a chance
And the rubbers sleep and the rulers don't make a peep
So now we all go to sleep.

Lauren Duncan (10)
Finzean Primary School, Finzean

SCHOOL

Monday morning has come
As I get off the bus
There are footballs flying across the fields,
The size of my head.

The bell rings at 9.15
We go into class
Look at the blackboard
That is the size of my head.

It starts to snow outside
Everyone goes as noisy as a hyena
Then the teacher starts to shout
To tell us all to be quiet.

Time for French at 2.00
Sometimes hard
Then it's maths,
The hardest of them all.

Then it's time to tidy up
For 2.30
Everyone tired, the class
As quiet as a mouse.

Rachel Lawson (10)
Finzean Primary School, Finzean

I Look Pretty, I Look Ugly

I look pretty, I look ugly
Pretty like a model
Ugly like a pig.

Wonderland is great, Wonderland is boring
Great like a theme park
Boring like school.

Pop stars are ace, pop stars are dumb
Ace like money
Dumb like maths.

Chocolate is yummy, chocolate is yucky
Yummy like sweeties
Yucky like veggies.

Holidays are hot, holidays are cold
Hot like Florida
Cold like Finzean.

My friends are cool, my friends are boring
Cool like TV
Boring like homework.

All these things are either pretty or ugly
Great or boring, ace or dumb, yummy or yucky
Hot or cold or cool.

Adèle Fraser (10)
Finzean Primary School, Finzean

My Home

This is my poem about my home
It's really warm and small
There's secrets behind every stone wall.

In the garden at my house
We have lots of flowers
Where little dickie birds sit looking for hours.

We live in the woods
It's where the squirrels nest
I bet the mighty oak tree is what they like the best.

Now round the back of the house
It's where the cars are parked
In the shed it's cold and very, very dark.

Mole holes next to the washing line
In my home it's where I feel fine
In my home everyone is kind.

The foxes hide in the trees
High above is the nest of buzzy bees
In the summer the trees are filled with fleas.

Now you know about my home
It's where I want to be
In the peace and quiet, just my family and me.

Ross Fazakerley-Guy (10)
Finzean Primary School, Finzean

THE DIGGER

My digger is slower than a turtle
My digger is as strong as a wall
My digger is hard as a truck
My digger smells like egg
My digger is as noisy as a drill
My digger is as big as a tank
Or an elephant on a double decker bus!

William Pattinson (8)
Finzean Primary School, Finzean

SHEEPDOG

My job all day is herding sheep
The days are long, there's little sheep.
When the day is finally through
I like to come home to you.

When I'm home I like to run and play
But the best thing of all was herding sheep
When I'm done the day starts again.

Alistair Ross (9)
Finzean Primary School, Finzean

DEAD RHINOS

Horns, horns so many horns
But where do they all come from?
Well I will tell you where
While I'm sitting here - it's rhinos!

Did you know?
Well I've told you now, it's poachers
Who kill with terrifying guns
For money. *Tut! Tut! Tut!*

Rumble! Rumble! Rumble! As the rhinos stampede.
Bang! Bang! Bang! As poachers kill
Saw! Saw! Saw! As poachers take off
The horns - rhinos destroyed.

As tall as a human.
As wide as a human and a half!
The rhino is dead, for horns, for money
Who would buy such things!

Callum Christie (9)
Finzean Primary School, Finzean

FOOTBALL CRAZY

Ruud
Gets his boots
Jaap gets his shinguard
Raul gets his gold, shiny boots
The red strip of Man United,
Excitement of a final
The sadness of losing at a final
The joy of winning the final
The players sweat dripping down
Mol's out for four years with a leg injury
Play practising ball skills
The shin pad as hard as a rock
Cantona shouts out, 'Ooh la la!'
Angus the bull walking in Pittodrie
Red Devil walking in Old Trafford
Scotland winning the World Cup
Jaap Stam gets his blue strip
Aberdeen win the
European Cup.

Andrew Littlejohn (10)
Finzean Primary School, Finzean

PANDA PANIC

Pandas are so very rare
And need a lot of care.
They live in the mountain's trees,
Of bamboo and china bees.
Then tragedy comes!
Pandas fleeing from their homes,
The fire, here it comes.
The smell of burning logs,
As the pandas gallop through squishy bogs
And the great river,
As they splash through they shiver.
Now they are on the other bank,
The fire as bright as the sun sank,
Into the rushing river.
Now it is a shiver
A shiver of relief
Now their coats are soft again,
As colour rushes through again,
Their cute faces are happy again,
But the bamboo forest will never be the same again!

Corrie Callander (10)
Finzean Primary School, Finzean

ELEPHANTS

All elephants on the plain live in a herd,
As the herd wander on swaying their long trunks
Feeling proud
A poacher came up and shot one elephant down.
The elephants look for waterholes to drink from
They suck water up their long trunks as long as string
The elephants keep going on and on
Looking out for danger, never do they stop
Only for a drink of water
To keep them going on and on.

Rory Farquharson (8)
Finzean Primary School, Finzean

ROMANS

R omans are strong
O r really, really tough
M en with swords, armour and shields
A ll the Romans charge and fight.
N ow they win, let's shout 'Hooray!'
S houting and screaming, some of them die.

Alexander Park (9)
Hayshead Primary School, Arbroath

BURNS

B urns used to write poems throughout the year
U nder a shelter or in a house
R ain is falling from the sky
N ow start to write
S uch good parties and poems on the day.

Kyle Geddes (9)
Hayshead Primary School, Arbroath

MY BROTHER

My brother is very boring
Yeah! We always fight everywhere
Brothers are a pain in the neck
Rather stupid, I would say
Out of the window I would go
They never ever let you play the PS2
He is always out with my football
Even though they are all right for some things
Roaring and roaring, that's all they do
He may not be perfect, but he is my brother.

Jordan Donaldson (9)
Hayshead Primary School, Arbroath

THE STORM

There was a storm
And there was rain
It was loud
On the windowpane
The wind was cold
I was blown away,
I fell over
And could not play.

Daniel McArdle (9)
Hayshead Primary School, Arbroath

SCHOOL

From Monday to Friday I get out of bed
Have my breakfast, then off to Hayshead
My mum tells me not to be a fool
And work hard when I'm at school
My mum and dad said if I do what they say
I will get a job and good pay
At night I like to play, have some fun
But not until my homework's done
When I have done all the above and been fed
That leaves one thing now, off to bed!

Alan Tallis (9)
Hayshead Primary School, Arbroath

MY DOG DARCEY

My dog Darcey
Likes his walk.
When I got his lead out
He barks and barks
When he gets in a bedroom
He jumps on the bed
When he gets in the car
He helps my dad drive
When I get his food out
He licks the tin
He's my very best pet
And I love him.

Jade Williamson (9)
Hayshead Primary School, Arbroath

MY MUM, DAD AND BROTHERS ARE PART OF GOD'S FAMILY

Yesterday we all had a 'family hour'
'Father, Father,' I said, 'won't you come down?'
After all this, I feel sorry for my family
Mum is mainly Dad's slave
I am his special daughter.
Lately I've been extremely sorry for the poor
You and your family should be too
I have served my God in a special way
Sometimes when I go to school, I start missing my family
Greeting people as we always do
Rainy days, we stay inside our houses
Every night in our house, we have to do homework
After school I spend time with my family
Today after school, I told my family that I loved them.

Kerry Louise Taylor (9)
Hayshead Primary School, Arbroath

HIDDEN TREASURES UNDER THE SEA

H idden treasures under the sea
I n the water, it's very cold
D own to the sea I go
D igging in the sea for treasure
E ver been down this far before?
'N ever,' my friend said.

T reasure chests full of gold
R eading the map to find the treasure
E ven you can read a map
A shark is going to eat us
S wim for your life!
U p there is the cave of treasure
R ead the map to find the door
E ver touched a fish before?

U p there I can see the door
N ow let's get some gold
D on't tell me there's a lock
E ver seen a lock like that?
R ivers can't be that good

T he cave is getting dark
H er torch went out
E ven she is scared

S een a shark in the cave
E ven I have seen a shark
A nd the torch went on again.

Josephine Dalziel (9)
Hayshead Primary School, Arbroath

A Special Friend For Me

F   riends are there for me, whenever
I   enjoy when we spend time together
E   njoying the day whilst we can, jump up and down.
N   ot very nice if she or he leaves you out.
D   ays are great, not good, but great
S   ummer is coming, days are longer.

A   nd it is so much fun when we play all together,
N   o it's not nice if you or me are all alone
D   ads are amusing when they play with you.

F   amilies are there for you and me,
A   friend is part of the family.
M   ums are so nice to you and me,
I   wish I had six or more mums, I think!
L   ove, they give to you and me
Y   es, they are all sweet and nice to be with.

Jamie Green (9)
Hayshead Primary School, Arbroath

MY KITTENS

M y kittens are fun,
Y ou would love them.

K ittens are cute,
I love them very much.
T he kittens are rascals
T he smallest one is okay
E verything about kittens is sweet.
N o they're not horrible,
S ome kittens fight.

Kayleigh Ross (9)
Hayshead Primary School, Arbroath

THE SUN

T he sun is hot
H igh above us
E arth is big

S pace is bigger than the sun
U nder the ground there are devils
N othing is hotter than the sun.

Jordan Tasker (10)
Hayshead Primary School, Arbroath

BROTHERS

B rothers I don't like them,
R otten brothers, who would have them?
O utside my brothers kick the football at my head
T hey are tell-tales
H ow they get so annoying, I don't know
E very morning they wake me up.
R unning away from my brothers would be cool.
S isters are the best.

Stacie Yeats (9)
Hayshead Primary School, Arbroath

MY CAT

My cat is playful
She's very funny
She catches fleas
And she see bunnies.
She annoys my sister when she's in bed,
She jumps on her and pats her head.
When I feed Kitty, she starts to purr
I stroke her on her cosy fur.

Caroline Watt (9)
Hayshead Primary School, Arbroath

MOTHER

M y mum is the best, she always gets a rest
O n schooldays my mum gives me sweets
T he toys she buys me are the best
H er hair is as black as coal
E very day my mum and dad are there for me
R hymes are her favourite.

Marc Walker (9)
Hayshead Primary School, Arbroath

MUM, DAD AND SISTER

My mum and dad are always there for me
They give me money
They might be mad at me, but they are not for long
I will always love my mum, dad and sister
I hope they love me too
They help me with my homework
My mum helps me with my spelling
My dad helps me with my maths
My mum, dad and sister mean the world to me!

Aimee Scott (9)
Hayshead Primary School, Arbroath

My Sister Is A Pest

M y sister is a pest
Y ou'd better not make a mess.

S o if you do, I'll make you wear a black dress,
I 'll tell Mum if you don't wear that black dress.
S isters are a pain in the neck
T elling lies all the time
E very single day she's bossy to me.
R ipping my hair out, bringing my smelly socks to me.

I get annoyed with sisters so much
S isters can be so boring sometimes.

A sister is okay sometimes when they are kind.

P erhaps I should be kind?
E very day I say, 'Go away!'
S o I started playing with her
T ill she stole my birthday toy, *oh no!*

Hayley Muldoon (9)
Hayshead Primary School, Arbroath

DISNEYLAND

D isneyland is great fun
I think the parks are brilliant
S unny days and warm nights
N ervous going on all the 'coasters
E very night late in bed
Y our feet get really sore

L eaving at ten o'clock in the morning
A lways having fun
N eeding drinks every half hour
D ays have gone and we're going home.

Conor Alexander Warren (9)
Hayshead Primary School, Arbroath

FOOTBALL

L arsson is the best
A h, he just scored!
R angers just scored
S utton scored, the score is 2-1
S ylla missed, oh no!
O h yes, another goal for Celtic.
N o team can beat Celtic.

Scott Webster (9)
Hayshead Primary School, Arbroath

SISTERS

S isters are the best
I love my sisters,
S isters help you every day
T he rascals they are
E mma is good.
'R ead me stories,' they say.
S isters are better than brothers!

Kara McLean (9)
Hayshead Primary School, Arbroath

THUNDER

I heard the thunder
The lightning struck a tree
It caught on fire
A crow went flying away
The antelope ran
The leaves were brown.
The rain fell heavily,
It was a scary night
I fell asleep
I dreamt of drums
When I woke up
The sun was out.

David Kelbie (9)
Hayshead Primary School, Arbroath

DREAM

On the hill, where the sweet grass grows,
The sun shines down as a gentle breeze blows.
The trees swish peacefully,
Animals live in harmony,
When the stars come out to play,
The hills are only a dream away.

Jade Anderson Hamilton (10)
Kinloch Primary School, Carnoustie

THE SEASHORE

The seashore has a big, blue sea
You can see it sparkle and glow.
The shells on the seashore are all different colours
Pink, red, green and blue.
The sand on the seashore is lemon-yellow
I feel it sliver between my toes.
The stones and pebbles are hard, but round
They smell like seaweed - but still, I love it.

Kirsty Strachan (10)
Kinloch Primary School, Carnoustie

HAIKU SEASONS

Spring

Yellow golden trees
Children running through the grass
Golden yellow trees.

Summer

Early morning day
Children playing on the beach
Laughing all day long.

Autumn

Brown bark on the trees
Children running through the leaves
Yellow leaves and brown.

Winter

Winter snow comes down
Covering the trees and leaves
Snowy winter day.

Sonya Finlayson (11)
Kinloch Primary School, Carnoustie

TOWNS

In the town
The cars go
Up and down
The busy, busy roads.
Passing by
The shops and buildings
Where people buy.
Post offices, buildings, libraries
And other places
All in a line.

Cara Steven (10)
Kinloch Primary School, Carnoustie

My Family

My mum is as funny as she can be
She always has time to talk to me,
When I came home
I'm never alone
Because I have my mum with me.

My dad is funny
He is better than the Easter bunny.
When it's time for tea
He's as happy as can be
He's the world's greatest.

My little sister Ellie
Loves to eat jelly
Sometimes she goes mad
But at least she's not being bad
That's my little sister Ellie.

I love my family.

Rebecca Anne Crabb (9)
Muirfield Primary School, Arbroath

MY FAMILY

My mum is very pretty and as funny as can be,
She's always there for me and makes me as happy as can be.
Me, I'm chatty and loud. I stand out from the crowd.
I wear stripy socks and Britney Spears rocks.
My brother Jakub is always in trouble,
Some days I wish I could put him in a bubble.
I really love him an awful lot,
But sometimes he loses the plot.

Rebekah-Jo Proctor (9)
Muirfield Primary School, Arbroath

MY FAVOURITE THINGS

My most favourite food is chips
And getting Brownie pips.
I like grey, fluffy kittens
And nice, woollen mittens.

I like letters in the post
And nice, hot, buttery toast
And cartoony ghosts
These are the things I like the most.

I like ice cream
And being in the netball team
I like being noisy, it's lots of fun
Especially when I get attention from everyone.

Nicole-Jayne Robertson (9)
Muirfield Primary School, Arbroath

Boo!

I hate spiders which lie in my room
Creeping silently through the night-time gloom.
Waiting until my eyes droop
Then coming down on their webs, doing loop-the-loop.
In my dreams the flowers wither
Then the spiders creep in and make me shiver.

I'm scared of my dad, who shouts at me
When I'm naughty he tells me what like I should be.
When he's angry, his eyes look as if they're red-hot,
He chases me round, waving a pot.
When he's furious, you're not even allowed to cough
When we go on an outing, he always tells me off.

I'm terrified of ghosts that are as white as a sheet
Clanking chains which are shiny and neat.
When they glide through my dream
I wake up and scream!
I hear them wailing, 'I'll get you!'
Then they creep up behind me and shout, *'Boo!'*

Samantha McLaren (9)
Muirfield Primary School, Arbroath

LIVING WORLD

Plants grow where the seeds land
Some grow in the jungle and some in your garden.

Sunflowers grow every year
Because every year when it gets cold
They scatter their seeds, very bold.

Trees are big plants - the daddy of the field.
Trees never die unless they are cut down.

All plants breathe in carbon dioxide
And breathe out oxygen

They're all photo synthesise.

Darren Muldoon (9)
Muirfield Primary School, Arbroath

FAMILY

My mum is pretty and she loves me
She is always happy when she cooks tea

My dad is happy as he can be
When he laughs at me he says, 'Hee, hee, hee!'

My sister loves me and her karaoke
But when she sings, she's not okay!

For me - I'm good and that's what I like
So that's what I'll be, even on my bike!

Robbie McKenzie (9)
Muirfield Primary School, Arbroath

FAVOURITE THINGS

My favourite thing is soccer,
I keep my football gear locked in a locker.

My favourite teams are Leeds United, Aberdeen, Arbroath
And not forgetting Manchester United.

My favourite players are Mark Viduka,
David Beckham and Davor Suker.

Daniel Thomas Reid (9)
Muirfield Primary School, Arbroath

MY IDOL

My idol is David Beckham
because he's good at his football.
He plays for Manchester United,
my favourite team.

He's one of my favourite players
because he also plays for England.
My favourite country.
He will always be my sporting idol.

Kevin Stewart (9)
Muirfield Primary School, Arbroath

MY ROOM

My room is special
It has lots of toys.
Everyone comes in it,
Except all the boys.

>My room is a tip,
>Toys everywhere.
>Except on my bed
>Which is just over there.

My room is pink and purple,
My room is on the right.
My room is really nice in the day,
But really safe and cosy at night.

Charis Skea (9)
Muirfield Primary School, Arbroath

MY ROOM

My room is the best
Better than the rest,
I play there with my friends,
With a fish stand that bends.

A computer is there too,
A fine one, I might say
Anyone for a DVD?
But no one's there to say.

I think the best thing is my PlayStation,
Better than the nation,
I've a very big stack of games,
With numerous names!

Thomas Irvine (9)
Muirfield Primary School, Arbroath

OCEAN DEEP FEARS

My biggest fear is an enormous shark with his big scales,
fins and sharp teeth.
He's the king of the ocean and has a bad temper.

My second biggest fear is an octopus, with its eight arms
and its purple skin.
He will grab you but he'll not fight, he'll eat you in one big bite.

My third and final fear is an eel, with his electric shocks,
He'll hurt you and burn you
If you try to fight him, you'll be sorry.

Steven Robert Boyd (9)
Muirfield Primary School, Arbroath

MY ROOM

My room is clean for now
I just don't know how!
I have a cosy bed
Where I lay my head
And I wake up in the morning.

I have a cuddly bear
With lots and lots of hair.
I have lots of toys
Which make a noise,
And I wake up in the morning.

I get my jammies on
And sing a little song,
As it gets dark
I fall asleep and think of the park
And I wake up in the morning.

Sam Ellis (9)
Muirfield Primary School, Arbroath

MY PETS

My pets are all birds
my biggest is called Buzz
she likes to ring her bell
and show off quite a lot.
She likes to climb her bars
all the way to the top.
She loves to eat her food
and loves to drink her water
and I am sure that she's the best bird ever.

Mitch Gillespie McDonald (9)
Muirfield Primary School, Arbroath

MY PET

My pet is called Larsson
He has sharp nails
He's very fluffy
But he's a bit scared

My brother has a guinea pig and it's called Ginger
He's got sharp nails
He's really fast at running
He's not very scared!

Scott Donald (9)
Muirfield Primary School, Arbroath

HOBBIES

I love horse riding
Fast, fast, fast.
Canter, trot
Run, run, run.

Over fences, I love to jump
Fast, fast, fast.
Canter, trot
Run, run, run.

I always have fun out in the fresh air
Fast, fast, fast.
Canter, trot
Run, run, run.

Doing jumps show style
Fast, fast, fast.
Canter, trot
Run, run, run.

Jodie Lana Noble (9)
Muirfield Primary School, Arbroath

MY ROOM

My bedroom is green
the best I have ever seen
It is like a green jellybean.
I have a white bed
with stripes of red
it's nice and soft for my head.
I have a green floor
and a brown door.
Tidying up is my chore.

Ryan Burnett (9)
Muirfield Primary School, Arbroath

FAVOURITE THINGS

My favourite things
are diamond rings
wearing them all day long
so come and sing this song

I also like to ride a bike
until it's night
where it's not that light.

What I love most
is beans on toast
so come along and
sing this wonderful song!

Bryony Joy Tait (9)
Muirfield Primary School, Arbroath

My Room

The reason I like my room
is that it's nice and quiet.
Sometimes I like to go in
my room to give myself
something to do.

Sometimes I get disturbed
by my sister, who barges in
whenever she likes.
I get annoyed and
I tell her to go away
and come back another day.

Calum Robert Grant (8)
Muirfield Primary School, Arbroath

POP STARS

I like pop stars
in fancy cars.

I love their songs
I could listen to them all day long.

The girls are slim
and the boys are trim.

Their jewellery shines
and their music chimes.

I like pop stars an awful lot!

Kelly-Louise Jamieson (9)
Muirfield Primary School, Arbroath

MY ROOM

My room is special
It makes me feel safe and warm.

Lots of toys to play with
Lots of games to choose from.

I like to sing in my room
Pretending I'm rich and famous.

With a blue carpet
Like the deep sea.

I always feel safe and relaxed.

Naomi Myles (8)
Muirfield Primary School, Arbroath

Man Utd

Man Utd are so great,
They are all so fine,
Veron, Beckham, Scholes and Giggs
Running all the time.

Bayer Leverkusen beat Man U
In the Champions League last year,
To celebrate getting this far,
They drank two bottles of beer.

They work as a team, every game
Passing really well.
They are second in the league this year,
But first is Arsenal.

Lloyd Ferguson (11)
St Ninian's Primary School, Dundee

BROTHERS RACING

I'm a really rapid racer
The best in all the world
The kid of rapid racer
That everyone can cuddle

I'm last in all the races
I'm always four minutes behind
I wish I could be better
But I'm really not that fine

I really am so great
Better than my brother
He never wins a race
Even ask my mother

Why can't I be as good?
My brother is so great
He beats me all the time
I just want to be the same!

Jamie Bray (11)
St Ninian's Primary School, Dundee

IN THE FUTURE

F uture times hold in store for us
U nderwater cars and a submarine bus.
T he adults will sit on a cloud to cry
U nusual green cows will be taught to fly
R ound the world, our holidays will be
E very year to Mercury.

Ruth Dundas (11)
St Ninian's Primary School, Dundee

POTIONS

Down, down, down in the deep, dark cave,
while the lightning turns the wave.
Witches polishing their own skulls,
normally witches are so dull.

As she turns towards the cauldron,
cauldron bubbles as it's burning.
Graveyard stone and foxes' bones
makes it scary on your own.

Cauldron screeches, smiling with fear,
hear the screeching in your ear.
Horse's tail and broomstick's end,
makes you go around the bend.

Potion is ready,
better watch out,
better get ready
to scream and shout!

Jacqueline Martinez (11)
St Ninian's Primary School, Dundee

MY RABBIT EDDIE

Rabbits *m*ay get a lot of love
especiall*y* when they're good

When *r*abbits are hungry
they get *a* bit jumpy
*b*ecause they don't have any food
they love eating ca*b*bage
They are magi*c*
Although their s*t*omach is full of baggage.

*E*veryone loves my little rabbit
But not when *d*ogs try to eat him
I love my E*d*die more than anything
When I look *i*nto his eyes and hold him close
It mak*e*s me feel happy.

Yazmin Hodgson (11)
St Ninian's Primary School, Dundee

STRAY

Scruffy, smelly, dripping wet,
She was always an unwanted pet.
Kids threw stones and kicked tin cans,
Some hit her with their filthy hands.

She scampered round the city streets,
Being trampled by the people's feet.
Until one day a little girl came
To the other kids, she wasn't the same.

She picked up the pussy, held her tight,
And took her home to bed that night.
She said that pussy is here to stay
But to some, she'll always be a stray.

Jemma Esposito (11)
St Ninian's Primary School, Dundee

THE SUN AND THE MOON

The sun shines so bright
It brings out some light,
The sun is a star
In the sky away far.

As the sun fades away
The moon comes out to play,
Ready for the night
With a glow, so bright.

The sun and the moon
Give us day and night,
They glow in the sky
Up above so high.

Kayesha Howett (11)
St Ninian's Primary School, Dundee

ORPHAN

Mary was alone, all on her own,
Shivering and shaking from head to toe.
It was dark there, cold there, isolated from all
Not even an insect would dare to crawl.
And she was alone, there was nowhere to go
But a shabby old alley, full of dustbins and rubbish.
A street-cleaner wouldn't even scrub it.
Rats were friends with this smelly, old place
And every time they smelled the food, they would race.
The moon shone down on the street,
But not even a beam would light up the alley.
Night fell and morning came,
But no one found her - no one claimed
To have lost a child who was smelly and plain.
She was on her own forever,
She didn't have any friends.
She didn't own much
But the clothes she was wearing, as such
No gifts for Christmas, no birthday presents she'd got
But was left to sit and beam up at what she had forgot.

Danielle Curran (10)
St Ninian's Primary School, Dundee

CAMPERDOWN ICE HOCKEY CLUB

C algary Flames wear the same logo as ours
A merican Hockey League
M ascot is a treat for a young supporter
P laying ice hockey is great fun
E very player is happy in our club
R acing to the top of the league
D angerous game to play
O ffside is what we try to avoid
W inning is the best feeling
N ational Hockey League

I ce skates are an important part of our kit
C hassis of our stick must be lightweight
E lbow pads are for protection

H ockey skills are what we learn at training
O n top of our game
C oyotes - the name of the our Under 12s
K illing the team on the scoreboard
E verlasting goals are what we want
Y oung team members are always joining

C amperdown are the best
L earning to play ice hockey
U nited in our game
B eating the other team is our aim.

Adam Barclay (10)
St Ninian's Primary School, Dundee

SCOTTISH WILDLIFE

A golden eagle is a majestic creature,
It flies so high
In Scotland's sky.
A red deer is a wonderful sight,
As it gazes quietly at the roadside.
I went to Arran to see the seals,
I could not believe this was real.
It was magnificent and the sight of them surreal.
The wildcat is very rare,
I bet you that no one would ever dare to stare.
I think Scottish wildlife is cool
That's why I'm writing this poem for school.

Alan Muhiddin (9)
St Ninian's Primary School, Dundee

RAINDROPS

If a kiss was a raindrop,
I'd send you showers.
If a hug was a second,
I'd send you hours.
If a smile was water
I'd send you the sea.
If a friend was a person,
I'd send you me.

Jamie Mackay (10)
St Ninian's Primary School, Dundee

MY BEST FOOTBALL PLAYER

When Henrik Larsson hits the ball
he always manages to score a goal.
When he runs around the pitch
he doesn't even get a stitch.
Oh Henrik, how do you do these things,
because you are the king of kings?
When he's offside there is never a doubt
netting hat-tricks, with his tongue hanging out.
Hey! Hey! Henrik, I want to know
oh how to you do those things?
When I see you with the ball at your feet
tearing past defenders it's such a treat!
You're so skilful you're so fine
I wish I could score every time!
Stand up tall, never look small,
magnificent number seven.
He keeps on scoring and we keep on singing,
when you do it, it sets the ball ringing.
Watching Celtic playing the best,
when they score -
it's the best feeling, I'll always adore.

Lewis Toshney (10)
St Ninian's Primary School, Dundee

THE RIVER

The red rose grows
by the river,
Children are having a picnic
and playing.
People are walking their dogs
some are on holiday,
A very beautiful day
by the river.

Rebecca McDonald (11)
St Ninian's Primary School, Dundee

BUSY DAY

Dawn has broken in the city of Dundee
the Tay sparkles under the rising sun,
People awake from their sleepy beds,
wondering is it going to be their day?

The roads are busy with traffic jams,
as people hurry to their jobs.
The bank's open with no time to spare
people come for cash, theirs
to spend until it's gone.

Evening has fallen and people sleep,
knowing tomorrow will be the same.
Alarms are ringing, morning has come
it's another day, it's got to be done.

Josh Forrester (11)
St Ninian's Primary School, Dundee

BIRTHDAY IN DISNEYLAND

It's my magical birthday, I am going to Disneyland
And I'll hear Donald Duck with his brass band.
There will be a dress-up party with Mickey Mouse and me
And my friend, we'll go sledding, until it's time for tea.
We'll play some games and we'll go to sleep,
And then I'll go home and get a lovely surprise
When my friends jump out and say, 'Surprise!'
Then my friends go home,
But something amazing happens!
I find a magic wand -
I can have another birthday tomorrow!

Charlotte Eggo (8)
Stracathro Primary School, Inchbare by Brechin

THE TIME MACHINE

There is a clock in the back of a shop
That has the power to make time stop
And start all over again.

I am telling you this story because it's absolutely gory
That made my life come to a grinding halt.

I went into that shop with the clock
That had the powers to make time stop
And didn't come out again!

What happened to me?
You wouldn't have liked to see.
It was too horrible even for me to tell you!

Innes Cuthill (8)
Stracathro Primary School, Inchbare by Brechin

THE DRAGON

It has large bat-like wings,
Made of hard, scaly things.
It has big, red, scary eyes,
They'll give you a nasty surprise.
It has fiery breath
It'll toast you to a crispy death!
It is ten times bigger than you or me,
But it really likes having a cup of tea!

Keenan Smith (9)
Stracathro Primary School, Inchbare by Brechin

THUMPER'S DAY OUT

One day I came home from school,
One day I saw a big hole in Thumper's run.
I thought, *where could he be?*
That little rat, running away from me!

Shaney Allan (9)
Stracathro Primary School, Inchbare by Brechin

THE MONSTER UNDER THE BED

I was scared of going to bed,
Because of what my dad said,
He played a trick on me
By making a noise that was scary
And certainly we did fall out.

I heard a noise, Dad wasn't there,
So I crawled into the monster's lair,
Met, did I and he
Got on well, did we,
And formed a revenge plan for Dad.

Going to bed I did not fear,
Dad thought it was rather queer.
When my dad went to bed,
'I feel scared!' he said,
For under his bed was the monster!

What the monster did I'll never know,
Maybe the monster bit Dad's big toe!
Or maybe bopped Dad's head,
Whilst he tried to sleep in bed,
Well, Dad never spoke of it again!

John Dalgarno (10)
Stracathro Primary School, Inchbare by Brechin

THE UNCONTROLLABLE TROLLEY!

I was in an awful hurry
I was in an awful flurry.
To get some food
That was really good,
But my squeaky wheels
Took me away from the deals
And into a very loud
Angry mob in the crowd.
I was starting to feel dizzy,
My head was going whizzy!
I ran into the cartons of soup
The soup definitely turned to gloop!
I unfortunately ran over a tin
I think the tin needed to go in the bin!
I bumped into the manager's hand
The manager's hand said that I was banned!
He told me to behave and *go!*
But it wasn't my fault, so I said *'No!'*
When I left, I wasn't jolly,
Because I had picked
The uncontrollable trolley!

Laura Cuthill (10)
Stracathro Primary School, Inchbare by Brechin

THE MONSTER THAT LIVES IN THE SEWER

'Never go in the sewer,' said Dad.
'Down there lives a monster who's mad.
He eats rats, cats, babies and bats
And likes to wear old, red hats.
He squeals when he makes big deals
And likes to smash up big bike wheels.
He likes to munch shoes with high heels
And has little worms with every meal.
He sits and plays the Nintendo all day
And then at night comes out to play.
He usually murders someone,
When he doesn't get his way.
So you'd better stay in until the break of day!'

Gareth Middleton (10)
Stracathro Primary School, Inchbare by Brechin

THE DEVIL

The Devil in the Forest of Cleaves,
He owns some pets of his.
Some of his traps are made of leaves,
He enjoys hurting people,
He's as scary as can be,
He messes up people's lives,
He can always see what's going on and
I really wish that he was gone.

Callum Leask (10)
Stracathro Primary School, Inchbare by Brechin

DOLPHINS

Dolphins can go very fast,
In a race they never come last.
They can get away from a shark
That comes out of the waters dark.

The water is smooth,
As they quickly move.
In a friendly pod
Eating plenty of cod.

They are extremely smart
Not at all like the boy called Bart.
They hardly ever seem to sleep,
Gliding through the ocean deep.

They have long bodies and a few fins,
Their teeth as sharp as pins.
High in the air they jump
And do not land with a thump.

Jenny August (10)
Stracathro Primary School, Inchbare by Brechin

MY CAT CALLED BILLY

I have a cat called Billy
Who really is quite silly
He has awful habits
Of eating too many rabbits
And when I go to bed
He'll sit up on his chair
Then I know he's safe and sound
When he's sleeping there.

When he wakes up in a big, big pile
He'll go down the stairs
Which takes him a while
Then goes out the cat flap, not in a rush
And walks past a bush which gives him a brush
He'll get to the corner and catches a mouse
Then drags him right in, right into the house!
Then comes into the living room
With his big, fat belly
And jumps on my lap while I'm watching the telly.

But that's only some days
He has other ways to play
'Cause when he gets bored on a wet winter day
He cuddles up by the fire, not in the mood to play
But rushes to me
Especially when he's needing his tea
Which will be gone in seconds.

Emma Ewen (9)
Stracathro Primary School, Inchbare by Brechin

THE BOOK REPORT

I was given a book report to do
    at home,
Just one problem, there was
    no book,
I knew I'd be in trouble if I
    didn't do it
I didn't feel hungry for the food
    that mum would cook.

Think, think, think of a book,
I left at school my rubber
    and pencil
I guess I'll have to make
    a book up,
Oh, it could be about a
    kitchen utensil.

I arrived at school, feeling very,
    very, nervous,
I walked into the playground of
    the big school,
Hoping that the teacher would
    believe in my report,
I didn't feel at all cool.

Shock, shock, running through
    my body,
Nineteen out of twenty, was
    my mark.
I really, really need
    to celebrate,
I think I'll have a party until
    it's dark.

So she really *had* believed me,
I got back the report from
      my teacher,
Maybe I could keep it for
      another time,
My teacher really was a
      gullible creature.

Alice McKenzie-Hodge (10)
Stracathro Primary School, Inchbare by Brechin

THE SNOWMAN

The snowman stared at the sky,
With a diamond twinkling in his eye,
As he saw his wife in the sky,
'Oh,' he said, 'I wish I could fly.'

He closed his eyes and wished as hard as he could,
Then suddenly he changed his mood
And floated straight up, as fast as he could,
Higher than a snowman should.

He was so happy when he met his mate,
That he gave her a box of After Eights.
Every year they go on this date
And they are never ever late.

Linzi Box (10)
Stracathro Primary School, Inchbare by Brechin

AIR TRAVEL

My air journey is going on and on,
Parents going nutty about their
growing lawns.
Poor green-faced Jill
Probably needs an air-sickness pill.

The stewardess was really tired,
She was worried about getting fired.
Children looking forward to hotels,
Parents say, 'If you want cheap *motels!*'

You can go to Asia
Or even somewhere in Malaysia.
Maybe, I like Dhaka, even Malacca.

Look out of the window and see the sky,
Looking at the clouds passing by.
There was nothing for me to see,
But there's a mini TV for me.

It's much better than sitting on gravel,
I think I like this air travel.
There was a madman who was
Yelling about his trunk,
I think he was a *bit* drunk.

I hate sitting with my sister,
She's like a nagging blister.
Mum says, 'Please don't fight!'
'Yeah, I'll push her off the flight.'

My parents are going crazy,
Not me, I'm soooo lazy.
I'm looking forward to my destination,
Air travel is a fascination!

Rima Puthu (11)
Stracathro Primary School, Inchbare by Brechin

THE BRILLIANT BIRTHDAY TRIP

On my eighth birthday, I had some
    friends to play.
I thought, *today is going to be magic*
    because it is my special day!
We looked under a panel on the
    kitchen floor
And suddenly we found a dusty,
    secret trapdoor.
So I thought bravely, *let's go in today!*

We went in and found a magic chair
    and you have to sit on its cushion -
    just there!
Then you can wish for anything that
    you want,
Even some bows and arrows to play
    'Hunt!'
You're not allowed any more than three,
    otherwise it isn't fair!

We stayed in there for two whole hours
    with lots of things to do
And, this may sound a little rude, but we
    couldn't find the loo!
Then my mum came looking for us,
    so I called to her to come in
And she said, 'Oh I knew it was you
    making that really loud din!
And I've made a birthday dinner,
    especially for you.'

'It's spaghetti for first, and for pudding
        it's ice cream
And for drinks, it's cola or lemonade
        which will surely make you gleam.'
Then Mum brought in my birthday cake and
        I blew the candles out
And then I saw my presents and
        I gave a great big *shout!*

Then after all this fuss, my stepdad James
        came into the kitchen and said,
'Did I miss anythin'?'

Huh! What's new?

Imogen Sherrit (8)
Stracathro Primary School, Inchbare by Brechin

OOR WULLIE

Oor Wullie
The Auchenshoogle king,
Sits on his bucket all day
And only comes off it to play.

Oor Wullie,
The Auchenshoogle king,
Has three friends,
Boab, Eck and Curly would go to the ends, with him.

Oor Wullie,
The Auchenshoogle king,
Has a dog called Hamish, a Scotty,
And a mouse called Jeemy, who's a wee bit naughty!

Ruari Box (11)
Stracathro Primary School, Inchbare by Brechin

SQUARE

Why am I a square?
Why am I a circle -
Or a shape like a pear?
Oh why am I a square?
And all because of that silly dare.

And all because of that silly dare,
I am now a fed up square.
Does no one care
For a square?

Eve Anderson (9)
Stracathro Primary School, Inchbare by Brechin